English
made easy

Key Stage 2
ages 9–10

Author
John Hesk

LONDON • NEW YORK • MUNICH • MELBOURNE • DELHI

More on plurals

Complete the following rules.

How to make plurals

1 For most **nouns**, simply add ....

2 If the **noun** ends with **-s**, **-sh** or **-ch**, add ....

3 For most **nouns** ending with an **-f**, change the **f** to ...., and then add ....

4 If the **noun** ends with **-ly**, **-ry** or **-ty**, change the .... to ...., and then add ....

5 If the **noun ends** with **-ay**, **-ey**, **-oy**, just add ....

Find examples of **nouns** that end in each of the ways described above.
Write the words as both **singular** and **plural** nouns.
Remember: A **noun** is a naming word.

1 ....

2 ....

3 ....

4 ....

5 ....

Peculiar plurals!

Add **-es** to these words.

potato ....   echo   ....   tomato ....

Add only **-s** to these words:

solo   ....   photo   ....   piano ....

Zulu   ....   banana ....   kiwi   ....

Word-building

Look carefully at the changes in these words.
    take – taking
    hope – hopeful
    love – lovely
    try – trying
    try – tries

Now complete this **spelling guide**.

When a word has a silent **-e** at the end, it usually loses this **-e** when we add

.... but keeps it when we add .... or ....

Before adding an **-s** to words that end in a **consonant** followed by **-y**, change the

.... to ....

Add **-ing** to these words. D

make + **-ing** becomes ....   flame + **-ing** becomes ....

move + **-ing** becomes ....   phone + **-ing** becomes ....

save + **-ing** becomes ....   dance + **-ing** becomes ....

Add **-ful** to these words. D

hope + **-ful** becomes ....   grace + **-ful** becomes ....

hate + **-ful** becomes ....   care + **-ful** becomes ....

use + **-ful** becomes ....   taste + **-ful** becomes ....

Add an **-s** to these words. Change the **-y** only if you need to. D

fly + **-s** becomes ....   dry + **-s** becomes ....

cry + **-s** becomes ....   multiply + **-s** becomes ....

carry + **-s** becomes ....   key + **-s** becomes ....

fry + **-s** becomes ....   assembly + **-s** becomes ....

Now write some **-ing**, **-ful** and **-s** words of your own. D

.... + **-ing** becomes .... + **-ing** becomes ....

.... + **-ful** becomes .... + **-ful** becomes ....

.... + **-s** becomes .... + **-s** becomes ....

More word-building

Do you know this verse?
> **i** *before* **e**,
> *Except after* **c**,
> *When the sound is* **ee**.

The words below follow this rule. Write the full word.

rec__ __ve ....

dec__ __ve ....

c__ __ling ....

f__ __ld ....

n__ __ce ....

p__ __r ....

ch__ __f ....

th__ __f ....

These words break the rule, so check in a **dictionary** before you write them.   D

s__ __ze ....

w__ __rd ....

spec__ __s ....

Match the following **prefixes** and **root words** to make new words. Then include each new word in a sentence.

Remember: A **prefix** is a group of letters added to the beginning of a word.

prefixes	roots	
in	regular	....
im	tect	....
ir	pend	....
pro	prove	....
sus	vent	....

....

....

....

....

....

Shortened words

Do you know the full forms of these **shortened names**?
Becky   Sue   Katie   Joe   Ben   Nick

Write the full names here in **alphabetical order**.

....

....

Here are some **shortened words**. Write their full version next to the short one.
Use a **dictionary** if you need help. D

bike   ....

bus   ....

fridge   ....

photo   ....

hippo   ....

o'clock   ....

phone   ....

Halloween   ....

plane   ....

pram   ....

rhino   ....

soccer   ....

Acronyms are words made from the first letters of words in longer phrases. Put the first letters of the words in these phrases together to make **acronyms**.

RAdio **D**etection **A**nd **R**anging is shortened to   *Radar*.................................

World **H**ealth **O**rganisation is shortened to   ....

Self **C**ontained **U**nderwater **B**reathing **A**pparatus is shortened to   ....

Personal **I**dentification **N**umber is shortened to   ....

Light **A**mplification by **S**timulated **E**mission of **R**adiation is shortened to   ....

Word origins

Many English words originally came from other languages. This means that these words often do not follow English spelling patterns. Look at the words below, and use a **dictionary** to find out which languages they originally came from. Then use your **dictionary** or another **reference book** to find where the languages are spoken. D

	Word	Language	Countries
1	anorak	....	....
2	koala	....	....
3	café	....	....
4	garage	....	....
5	kayak	....	....
6	lieutenant	....	....
7	mayonnaise	....	....
8	sushi	....	....
9	judo	....	....
10	beret	....	....
11	hamburger	....	....
12	spaghetti	....	....
13	khaki	....	....
14	karate	....	....
15	bungalow	....	....
16	ketchup	....	....
17	yoghurt	....	....
18	teepee	....	....
19	restaurant	....	....
20	algebra	....	....

Onomatopoeia

The words below have **sounds** that match their meanings.
Remember: When the sound of a word connects with its meaning, it is
called **onomatopoeic**.

splash   crash   smash   clash

clatter   plop   clap

gurgle   snap   buzz   rumble

tinkle   click   whir   tick

bang   roar   squeal

Match the **sound words** above to the different situations below. Write the relevant **sound
word** in the appropriate box. Add some more **sound words** of your own if you wish!

Thunderstorm *crash*

Sports day

In the swimming pool

In the kitchen

7

Prepositions

Here are some useful **prepositions**:

at   by   for   from   in   of   off   on   through   to   up   with

inside   outside   after   towards   underneath   across   except   between

A **preposition** is missing from each of the following sentences. Choose the one that fits best from the list, and write it in the space. You may find that more than one could fit.
Remember: A **preposition** is placed before a word to connect it to other words in a sentence.

The power button was .... the CD drive.

She aimed .... the target.

The ball went .... the window.

I climbed .... the ladder.

Try to hit the ball .... the bat.

We went .... the house when it started to rain.

The cat was hiding .... the bed.

It is one .... the most exciting films I've ever seen.

It's just one thing .... another!

Let's go .... a swim.

Now write ten sentences of your own, using the remaining **prepositions** in the list.

....

....

....

....

....

....

....

....

....

....

Soft c and homophones

All the **definitions** below are of words that begin with **ci-**. The letter **c** sounds like an **s** when these words are spoken. Use a **dictionary** to help you find the words that fit the **definitions**. D

a drink made from apples ....

a partly burned fuel such as coal ....

a character in a fairy tale ....

where films are shown ....

a spice ....

a shape ....

the distance round a circle ....

a travelling show ....

a large town ....

polite ....

The words below sound the same, but are spelt differently and have different meanings. They are called **homophones**.

great and grate   paws, pores and pause   rain, rein and reign

Can you find a **homophone** for each of these words?

awe ....   bear ....

ceiling ....   draft ....

eight ....   fare ....

guest ....   hare ....

inn ....   bye ....

wait ....   sea ....

pare ....   feet ....

Reading a text

Read this **text**, then answer the questions in full sentences.

The Voice of Nature

An Aboriginal myth from southern Australia relates how, in the beginning, the voice of the Ancestor spoke each day from a great gum tree, and the tribe gathered around to listen. But as time went by the people grew weary of hearing his words of wisdom. One by one they turned their backs on the voice to pursue their own pleasures, and a vast silence settled over the whole of the land and the sea. There was no wind and the tides were still, no birds sang, and the earth seemed to be dying.

The tribe soon wearied of the pleasures of their own making and began to be afraid and lonely. They returned to the great tree again and again, hoping to hear the words that would ease their misery. And one day the voice of their Ancestor spoke again.

He told them it was the last time his voice would be heard, but that he would give them a sign. The great tree split open, a huge tongue of light came down into its trunk, and then it closed up again.

Since that time the Aboriginals have known that the voice of their Ancestor exists in all things, and speaks to them through every part of nature.

From *Dreamtime Heritage* by A. & M. J. Roberts

Why did the tribe traditionally gather around the great gum tree?

....

....

Why did the people abandon this custom (stop going to the tree)?

....

....

What happened to the natural world when the people broke this tradition?

....

....

What feelings made the people return to the tree?

....

....

Reading and understanding

Reread the **text** on page 10, then answer the following questions in full sentences.

What is an **ancestor**? ☐D

....

....

Describe the sign given to the people by the Ancestor. Explain the meaning of the sign.

....

....

....

The Australian gum tree has a **scientific** name. Use **reference books** or a **computer** to find out what it is, and write it here.

....

Explain the word **tribe**. What do we mean by **tribal society**? ☐D

....

....

What evidence can you find in the text to suggest that **nature** was important to the people? Can you explain why this was?

....

....

Gum trees will grow again after they have burnt to the ground. Do you think this fact might be connected with the story?

....

....

....

Use a **dictionary** to find out what the saying "up a gum tree" means. ☐D

....

....

....

A traditional story

Read this **story** from India about a tree, and answer the questions in full sentences. The writer explains that, as a child, she often heard this story told on a special day in March – the Day for Brothers – when "all sisters in India pray that no harm comes to their brothers".

The Mango Tree (Part One)

In a small town, there was a small house in which lived a young man, his wife, and the young man's sister. This small house had a small garden at the back in which grew a small mango tree. One day the young man's wife came to him and said, "Look here, I'm fed up with our situation. Your sister …"

"Have you come here to complain about my sister again?"

"What can I do? I know it's quite useless … My complaints fall on deaf ears, anyway … I'm just … so angry with your sister. I get up early in the morning, draw water from the well, light the fire in the kitchen, cook breakfast, wash and scrub pots …"

"Don't go on," said the brother. "I've heard it all before."

"And what does your lazy sister do all day? Nothing … nothing … she lolls about in the garden, watering her mango tree, talking to it, clearing away dead leaves, and feeding it manure and mulch …"

"That isn't all she does. She comes in and talks to me. Just an hour ago, she was playing chess with me."

"Just because she adores you, doesn't mean you should ignore her faults. You must tell her to leave that … silly mango tree alone, and come and help me with the housework. I really think we should marry her off. That might teach her to be more responsible."

Since the sister was of marriageable age, the brother could not really object. He knew though, that he would miss her very, very much.

A marriage was arranged.

Why did the young man's wife complain to him?

....

....

What does the writer mean when she writes that the marriage was arranged?

....

....

Now read part two of the **story** that began on page 12, then answer the questions.

The Mango Tree (Part Two)

When all the ceremonies were over, and the sister was about to leave with her groom to lead a new life in a new town, she turned to her sister-in-law and said, "Dearest sister-in-law, I'm going to miss my mango tree so much. Would you please do me a great favour and look after it for me? Please water it well and clear the weeds that grow in its shadow."

"Oh, well, yes, yes," answered the sister-in-law.

Once the sister had left, the sister-in-law turned to her husband and yelled, "Did you hear that? Did you *hear* that? Did you hear your selfish sister? She didn't say that she was going to miss you. She didn't say that she was going to miss me. She *did* say that she was going to miss her mango tree!" She decided then that she was going to ignore the mango tree. The mango tree irritated her just as much as her husband's sister had. Now she could be rid of both.

As the days passed, the unwatered, uncared for mango tree started drying up and its leaves began to fall.

At the same time, the brother, who had been a strong, robust and healthy young man, began to lose his appetite and get thinner and weaker.

One day, a letter arrived. It was from the sister and said, "Dearest brother and sister-in-law. I hope all is well and that my tree is green, and that my brother is in good health."

The remaining leaves of the mango tree were quite yellow by this time, but the sister-in-law wrote back, "Dearest sister. Your tree is fine, but your brother has not been feeling so good."

Soon another letter arrived from the sister. "Are you sure my tree is green? And how is my brother?"

Why did the young man's wife object when his sister said that she would miss her mango tree?

....

....

Explain why the young man's wife neglected the tree.

....

....

A traditional story (continued)

Read part three of the **story**, then answer the questions.

The Mango Tree (Part Three)

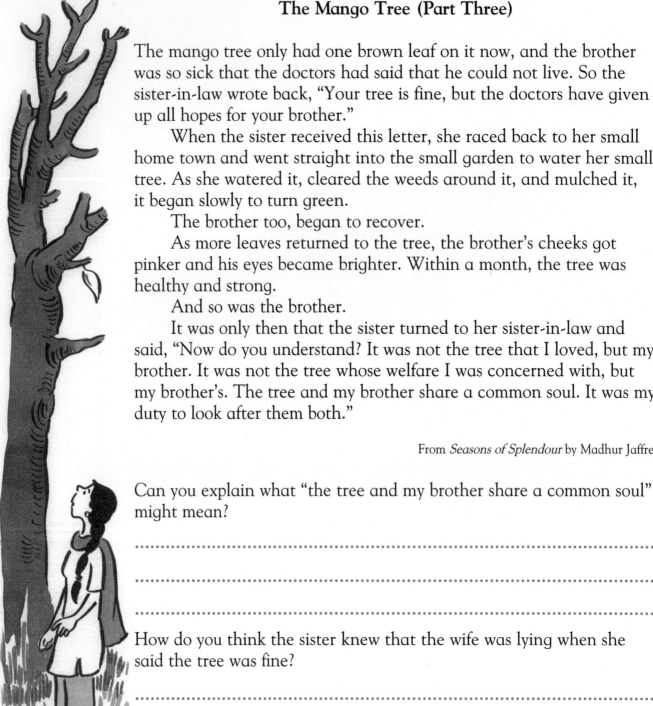

The mango tree only had one brown leaf on it now, and the brother was so sick that the doctors had said that he could not live. So the sister-in-law wrote back, "Your tree is fine, but the doctors have given up all hopes for your brother."

When the sister received this letter, she raced back to her small home town and went straight into the small garden to water her small tree. As she watered it, cleared the weeds around it, and mulched it, it began slowly to turn green.

The brother too, began to recover.

As more leaves returned to the tree, the brother's cheeks got pinker and his eyes became brighter. Within a month, the tree was healthy and strong.

And so was the brother.

It was only then that the sister turned to her sister-in-law and said, "Now do you understand? It was not the tree that I loved, but my brother. It was not the tree whose welfare I was concerned with, but my brother's. The tree and my brother share a common soul. It was my duty to look after them both."

From *Seasons of Splendour* by Madhur Jaffrey

Can you explain what "the tree and my brother share a common soul" might mean?

....

....

....

How do you think the sister knew that the wife was lying when she said the tree was fine?

....

....

....

Of the three characters in this **story**, whose opinions and feelings do we learn most about?

....

....

Your own story

Reread the **story** on pages 12, 13 and 14, then choose either the brother or the sister, and **retell** the **story** from his or her **point of view**. You might find it easier if you imagine that you are the **character** you have chosen.

Add extra details if you like, but do not change the main point of the **story** or what happens.

Possessive apostrophes

A **possessive apostrophe** shows us who or what belongs to somebody or something.

We usually write **the brothers of Madhur** as **Madhur's brothers**, and we write **the sister of the brothers** as **the brothers' sister**.

The **apostrophe** is always placed after the word that is "owning". Add an **-s** if it **sounds** necessary.

Write **the friend of Thomas** as **Thomas's friend**.

Rewrite the **phrases** below so that they include a **possessive apostrophe**. The first one has been done for you.

the mango tree of his sister   *his sister's mango tree*

the wives of the men   ....

the beliefs of the tribe   ....

the fruit of the trees   ....

the wisdom of the Ancestor   ....

the roots of the mango tree   ....

the saris of the women   ....

the opinion of my sister   ....

the branches of the tree   ....

the laughter of the children   ....

These **phrases** work in the same way, although you might not think so! Rewrite them.

in the time of three days   *in three days' time*

in the time of one hour   ....

in the time of two weeks   ....

Answer Section with Parents' Notes

Key Stage 2
Ages 9–10

This 8-page section provides answers or explanatory notes to all the activities in this book. This will enable you to assess your child's work.

Point out any spelling mistakes, incorrect punctuation and grammatical errors as you mark each page. Also correct any handwriting errors. (Your child should use the handwriting style taught at his or her school.) As well as making corrections, it is very important to praise your child's efforts and achievements.

Encourage your child to use a dictionary, and suggest that he or she uses a notebook to compile a **word bank** of new words or difficult spellings.

More on plurals

Complete the following rules.

How to make plurals

1 For most **nouns**, simply add _s_ .

2 If the **noun** ends with **-s, -sh** or **-ch**, add _es_ .

3 For most **nouns** ending with an **-f**, change the **f** to _v_ , and then add _es_ .

4 If the **noun** ends with **-ly, -ry** or **-ty**, change the _y_ to _ie_ , and then add _s_ .

5 If the **noun** ends with **-ay, -ey, -oy**, just add _s_ .

Find examples of **nouns** that end in each of the ways described above. Write the words as both **singular** and **plural** nouns.
Remember: A noun is a naming word.

1 ....

2 ....

3 .... Answers may vary ....

4 ....

5 ....

Peculiar plurals!
Add **-es** to these words.

potato _potatoes_   echo _echoes_   tomato _tomatoes_

Add only **-s** to these words:

solo _solos_   photo _photos_   piano _pianos_

Zulu _Zulus_   banana _bananas_   kiwi _kiwis_

This page focuses on five general rules that will help your child to form plurals. The final activity features a number of common words that do not follow these rules.

Word-building

Look carefully at the changes in these words.
take – taking
hope – hopeful
love – lovely
try – trying
try – tries

Now complete this **spelling guide**.

When a word has a silent **-e** at the end, it usually loses this **-e** when we add _ing_ but keeps it when we add _ful_ or _ly_ .

Before adding an **-s** to words that end in a **consonant** followed by **-y**, change the _y_ to _ie_ .

Add -ing to these words. D

make + **-ing** becomes _making_   flame + **-ing** becomes _flaming_

move + **-ing** becomes _moving_   phone + **-ing** becomes _phoning_

save + **-ing** becomes _saving_   dance + **-ing** becomes _dancing_

Add -ful to these words. D

hope + **-ful** becomes _hopeful_   grace + **-ful** becomes _graceful_

hate + **-ful** becomes _hateful_   care + **-ful** becomes _careful_

use + **-ful** becomes _useful_   taste + **-ful** becomes _tasteful_

Add an -s to these words. Change the -y only if you need to. D

fly + **-s** becomes _flies_   dry + **-s** becomes _dries_

cry + **-s** becomes _cries_   multiply + **-s** becomes _multiplies_

carry + **-s** becomes _carries_   key + **-s** becomes _keys_

fry + **-s** becomes _fries_   assembly + **-s** becomes _assemblies_

Now write some **-ing, -ful** and **-s** words of your own. D

.... + **-ing** becomes .... + **-ing** becomes ....

.... + **-ful** becomes _Answers may vary_ **-ful** becomes ....

.... + **-s** becomes .... + **-s** becomes ....

This page uses word-building as an aid to spelling. Make sure that your child has completed and understood the two rules at the top of the page before he or she begins the exercises below. Encourage your child to check his or her answers in a dictionary.

More word-building

Do you know this verse?
i *before* e,
Except after c,
When the sound is ee.

The words below follow this rule. Write the full word.

rec _e_ i ve _receive_   n i _e_ ce _niece_

dec _e_ i ve _deceive_   p i _e_ r _pier_

c _e_ i ling _ceiling_   ch i _e_ f _chief_

f i _e_ ld _field_   th i _e_ f _thief_

These words break the rule, so check in a **dictionary** before you write them. D

s _e_ i ze _seize_

w _e_ i rd _weird_

spec i _e_ s _species_

Match the following **prefixes** and **root words** to make new words. Then include each new word in a sentence.
Remember: A prefix is a group of letters added to the beginning of a word.

prefixes	roots	
in	regular	_invent_
im	tect	_improve_
ir	pend	_irregular_
pro	prove	_protect_
sus	vent	_suspend_

....

....

.... Answers may vary ....

....

Check that your child knows and understands the verse. Use the word *chief* to show that the rule applies to the *ee* sound only when it immediately follows *c*. Learning the meanings of common prefixes and roots will also improve your child's spelling.

Shortened words

Do you know the full forms of these **shortened names**?
Becky Sue Katie Joe Ben Nick

Write the full names here in **alphabetical order**.
Benjamin, Joseph, Katherine, Nicholas, Rebecca, Susan

Here are some **shortened words**. Write their full version next to the short one.
Use a **dictionary** if you need help. [D]

bike — bicycle
bus — omnibus

fridge — refrigerator
photo — photograph

hippo — hippopotamus
o'clock — of the clock

phone — telephone
Halloween — Allhallows Eve

plane — aeroplane
pram — perambulator

rhino — rhinoceros
soccer — Association football

Acronyms are words made from the first letters of words in longer phrases. Put the first letters of the words in these phrases together to make **acronyms**.

RAdio Detection And Ranging is shortened to — Radar

World Health Organisation is shortened to — WHO

Self Contained Underwater Breathing Apparatus is shortened to — Scuba

Personal Identification Number is shortened to — PIN

Light Amplification by Stimulated Emission of Radiation is shortened to — Laser

The fun activities on this page allow your child to find out how short words are created from longer words and phrases. Talk about the "living" nature of languages – how languages change and develop.

Word origins

Many English words originally came from other languages. This means that these words often do not follow English spelling patterns. Look at the words below, and use a **dictionary** to find out which languages they originally came from. Then use your **dictionary** or another **reference book** to find where the languages are spoken. [D]

	Word	Language	Countries
1	anorak	Inuit	Greenland
2	koala	Aboriginal	Australia
3	café	French	France
4	garage	French	France
5	kayak	Inuit	Greenland
6	lieutenant	French	France
7	mayonnaise	French	France
8	sushi	Japanese	Japan
9	judo	Japanese	Japan
10	beret	French	France
11	hamburger	German	Germany
12	spaghetti	Italian	Italy
13	khaki	Urdu	Persia (Iran)
14	karate	Japanese	Japan
15	bungalow	Hindi	India, Bangladesh
16	ketchup	Chinese	China
17	yoghurt	Turkish	Turkey
18	teepee	Siouan	North America
19	restaurant	French	France
20	algebra	Arabic	Saudi Arabia, Kuwait, etc

Pages 6 and 7 encourage your child to look at English words that originate from other languages. Some dictionaries may disagree with these answers – explain that it can be difficult to determine a word's exact origin, but that this makes the "detective work" fun.

Onomatopoeia

The words below have **sounds** that match their meanings.
Remember: When the sound of a word connects with its meaning, it is called **onomatopoeic**.

splash crash smash clash
clatter plop clap
gurgle snap buzz rumble
tinkle click whir tick
bang roar squeal

Match the **sound words** above to the different situations below. Write the relevant **sound word** in the appropriate box. Add some more **sound words** of your own if you wish!

| Thunderstorm | crash, splash, smash, clash, plop, gurgle, snap, rumble, bang, roar |

| Sports day | clap, buzz, bang, roar, squeal |

| In the swimming pool | splash, clatter, plop, gurgle |

| In the kitchen | splash, clatter, plop, gurgle, tinkle, tick, whir, click |

The activity on this page revises your child's understanding of onomatopoeia. Check his or her choices for each box, and comment on any further words he or she has suggested, discussing how appropriate they are and if they are spelt correctly.

Prepositions

Here are some useful **prepositions**.
at by for from in of off on through to up with
inside outside after towards underneath across except between

A **preposition** is missing from each of the following sentences. Choose the one that fits best from the list, and write it in the space. You may find that more than one could fit.
Remember: A **preposition** is placed before a word to connect it to other words in a sentence.

The power button was — underneath — the CD drive..

She aimed — at — the target.

The ball went — through — the window.

I climbed — up — the ladder.

Try to hit the ball — with — the bat.

We went — inside — the house when it started to rain.

The cat was hiding — underneath — the bed.

It is one — of — the most exciting films I've ever seen.

It's just one thing — after — another!

Let's go — for — a swim.

Now write ten sentences of your own, using the remaining **prepositions** in the list.

Answers may vary

These exercises will help your child to appreciate the wide range of prepositions and to understand their function in sentences. Talk about your child's sentences to consolidate his or her understanding and knowledge.

Soft c and homophones

All the **definitions** below are of words that begin with **ci-**. The letter **c** sounds like an **s** when these words are spoken. Use a **dictionary** to help you find the words that fit the **definitions**. [D]

a drink made from apples _cider_

a partly burned fuel such as coal _cinder_

a character in a fairy tale _Cinderella_

where films are shown _cinema_

a spice _cinnamon_

a shape _circle_

the distance round a circle _circumference_

a travelling show _circus_

a large town _city_

polite _civil_

The words below sound the same, but are spelt differently and have different meanings. They are called **homophones**.

great and grate   paws, pores and pause   rain, rein and reign

Can you find a **homophone** for each of these words?

awe	_ore_	bear	_bare_
ceiling	_sealing_	draft	_draught_
eight	_ate_	fare	_fair_
guest	_guessed_	hare	_hair_
inn	_in_	bye	_by_
wait	_weight_	sea	_see_
pare	_pair_	feet	_feat_

Ensure that your child knows that the letter *c* can sometimes sound like *s*. Can your child think of any more words with the soft *c* sound? The second exercise looks at homophones. Help your child find homophones for all the words in the list.

Reading a text

Read this **text**, then answer the questions in full sentences.

The Voice of Nature

An Aboriginal myth from southern Australia relates how, in the beginning, the voice of the Ancestor spoke each day from a great gum tree, and the tribe gathered around to listen. But as time went by the people grew weary of hearing his words of wisdom. One by one they turned their backs on the voice to pursue their own pleasures, and a vast silence settled over the whole of the land and the sea. There was no wind and the tides were still, no birds sang, and the earth seemed to be dying.

The tribe soon wearied of the pleasures of their own making and began to be afraid and lonely. They returned to the great tree again and again, hoping to hear the words that would ease their misery. And one day the voice of their Ancestor spoke again.

He told them it was the last time his voice would be heard, but that he would give them a sign. The great tree split open, a huge tongue of light came down into its trunk, and then it closed up again.

Since that time the Aboriginals have known that the voice of their Ancestor exists in all things, and speaks to them through every part of nature.

From *Dreamtime Heritage* by A. & M. J. Roberts

Why did the tribe traditionally gather around the great gum tree?
The tribe used to gather around the great gum tree to hear the Ancestor speak.

Why did the people abandon this custom (stop going to the tree)?
They abandoned this custom because they grew weary of hearing the Ancestor's
words of wisdom.

What happened to the natural world when the people broke this tradition?
When the people broke this tradition there was no wind or tides, no birds sang,
and the earth seemed to be dying.

What feelings made the people return to the tree?
Feelings of fear and lonliness made the people return to the tree.

The National Literacy Strategy requires your child to examine a range of texts from different cultures. Listen to your child read the extract, and help him or her with difficult words. Then discuss the customs and beliefs of this tribe.

Reading and understanding

Reread the **text** on page 10, then answer the following questions in full sentences.

What is an **ancestor**? [D]
An ancestor is someone from whom a person is descended.

Describe the sign given to the people by the Ancestor. Explain the meaning of the sign.
The great tree split open, a huge tongue of light came down into its trunk, and
then it closed up again. This was a sign that the Ancestor is present in all
things and speaks to the people through every part of nature.

The Australian gum tree has a **scientific** name. Use **reference books** or a **computer** to find out what it is, and write it here.
Eucalyptus

Explain the word **tribe**. What do we mean by **tribal society**? [D]
A tribe is a group of people with common ancestors. Tribal society is a society
organised 'around' the culture and rules of a tribe.

What evidence can you find in the text to suggest that **nature** was important to the people? Can you explain why this was?
The people felt afraid and lonely when the earth seemed to be dying.
They gathered round the gum tree every day to listen to their Ancestor.

Gum trees will grow again after they have burnt to the ground. Do you think this fact might be connected with the story?
Yes. In the story, the tree splitting and the tongue of
light could describe a lightning strike.

Use a **dictionary** to find out what the saying "up a gum tree" means. [D]
The saying "up a gum tree" means to be in a very
awkward or difficult position.

The questions on this page refer to the extract on page 10. Encourage your child to develop good research skills. He or she could use reference books, CD-ROMs or the Internet, which should all be available at your local library.

A traditional story

Read this **story** from India about a tree, and answer the questions in full sentences. The writer explains that, as a child, she often heard this story told on a special day in March – the Day for Brothers – when "all sisters in India pray that no harm comes to their brothers".

The Mango Tree (Part One)

In a small town, there was a small house in which lived a young man, his wife, and the young man's sister. This small house had a small garden at the back in which grew a small mango tree. One day the young man's wife came to him and said, "Look here, I'm fed up with our situation. Your sister …"

"Have you come here to complain about my sister again?"

"What can I do? I know it's quite useless … My complaints fall on deaf ears, anyway … I'm just … so angry with your sister. I get up early in the morning, draw water from the well, light the fire in the kitchen, cook breakfast, wash and scrub pots …"

"Don't go on," said the brother. "I've heard it all before."

"And what does your lazy sister do all day? Nothing … nothing … she lolls about in the garden, watering her mango tree, talking to it, clearing away dead leaves, and feeding it manure and mulch …"

"That isn't all she does. She comes in and talks to me. Just an hour ago, she was playing chess with me."

"Just because she adores you, doesn't mean you should ignore her faults. You must tell her to leave that … silly mango tree alone, and come and help me with the housework. I really think we should marry her off. That might teach her to be more responsible."

Since the sister was of marriageable age, the brother could not really object. He knew though, that he would miss her very, very much.

A marriage was arranged.

Why did the young man's wife complain to him?
She complained because the young man's sister did nothing all
day except care for the mango tree.

What does the writer mean when she writes that the marriage was arranged?
The sister's marriage was arranged by her brother and sister-
in-law. They chose the groom and organised the wedding.

Pages 12 to 15 provide your child with a further opportunity to investigate text from another culture. The text is quite long, and your child may need help and encouragement. It may help if you read the story together and then discuss its content.

Now read part two of the **story** that began on page 12, then answer the questions.

The Mango Tree (Part Two)

When all the ceremonies were over, and the sister was about to leave with her groom to lead a new life in a new town, she turned to her sister-in-law and said, "Dearest sister-in-law, I'm going to miss my mango tree so much. Would you please do me a great favour and look after it for me? Please water it well and clear the weeds that grow in its shadow."

"Oh, well, yes, yes," answered the sister-in-law.

Once the sister had left, the sister-in-law turned to her husband and yelled, "Did you hear that? Did you *hear* that? Did you hear your selfish sister? She didn't say that she was going to miss you. She didn't say that she was going to miss me. She *did* say that she was going to miss her mango tree!" She decided then that she was going to ignore the mango tree. The mango tree irritated her just as much as her husband's sister had. Now she could be rid of both.

As the days passed, the unwatered, uncared for mango tree started drying up and its leaves began to fall.

At the same time, the brother, who had been a strong, robust and healthy young man, began to lose his appetite and get thinner and weaker.

One day, a letter arrived. It was from the sister and said, "Dearest brother and sister-in-law. I hope all is well and that my tree is green, and that my brother is in good health."

The remaining leaves of the mango tree were quite yellow by this time, but the sister-in-law wrote back, "Dearest sister. Your tree is fine, but your brother has not been feeling so good."

Soon another letter arrived from the sister. "Are you sure my tree is green? And how is my brother?"

Why did the young man's wife object when his sister said that she would miss her mango tree?
The man's wife felt that his sister cared more about the
tree than she cared about them.

Explain why the young man's wife neglected the tree.
She neglected the tree because she was annoyed with her
sister-in-law and the fuss she had made of the tree.

Check your child's understanding of the story by discussing it. Talk about the portrayal of the young man's wife – are her feelings and actions understandable? Ask your child what he or she thinks is likely to happen next.

A traditional story (continued)

Read part three of the **story**, then answer the questions.

The Mango Tree (Part Three)

The mango tree only had one brown leaf on it now, and the brother was so sick that the doctors had said that he could not live. So the sister-in-law wrote back, "Your tree is fine, but the doctors have given up all hopes for your brother."

When the sister received this letter, she raced back to her small home town and went straight into the small garden to water her small tree. As she watered it, cleared the weeds around it, and mulched it, it began slowly to turn green.

The brother too, began to recover.

As more leaves returned to the tree, the brother's cheeks got pinker and his eyes became brighter. Within a month, the tree was healthy and strong.

And so was the brother.

It was only then that the sister turned to her sister-in-law and said, "Now do you understand? It was not the tree that I loved, but my brother. It was not the tree whose welfare I was concerned with, but my brother's. The tree and my brother share a common soul. It was my duty to look after them both."

From Seasons of Splendour by Madhur Jaffrey

Can you explain what "the tree and my brother share a common soul" might mean?
It might mean that the tree and the brother were somehow
connected.

How do you think the sister knew that the wife was lying when she said the tree was fine?
The sister knew that the wife was lying because the tree couldn't
be fine if her brother was dying.

Of the three characters in this **story**, whose opinions and feelings do we learn most about?
We learn most about the opinions and feelings of the wife.

Discuss the connection between the brother and the mango tree. What does your child think of this part of the story? It may help if you discuss the questions before your child writes his or her answers.

Your own story

Reread the **story** on pages 12, 13 and 14, then choose either the brother or the sister, and **retell** the **story** from his or her **point of view**. You might find it easier if you imagine that you are the **character** you have chosen.

Add extra details if you like, but do not change the main point of the **story** or what happens.

Answers may vary

Your child's story should be narrated by the brother or sister or told from his or her point of view. The National Literacy Strategy requires your child to understand that stories can be told from different points of view and that these may influence the reader.

Possessive apostrophes

A **possessive apostrophe** shows us who or what belongs to somebody or something.

We usually write **the brothers of Madhur** as **Madhur's brothers**, and we write **the sister of the brothers** as **the brothers' sister**.

The **apostrophe** is always placed after the word that is "owning". Add an **-s** if it **sounds** necessary.

Write **the friend of Thomas** as **Thomas's friend**.

Rewrite the **phrases** below so that they include a **possessive apostrophe**. The first one has been done for you.

the mango tree of his sister	his sister's mango tree
the wives of the men	the men's wives
the beliefs of the tribe	the tribe's beliefs
the fruit of the trees	the trees' fruit
the wisdom of the Ancestor	the Ancestor's wisdom
the roots of the mango tree	the mango tree's roots
the saris of the women	the women's saris
the opinion of my sister	my sister's opinion
the branches of the tree	the tree's branches
the laughter of the children	the children's laughter

These **phrases** work in the same way, although you might not think so! Rewrite them.

in the time of three days	in three days' time
in the time of one hour	in one hour's time
in the time of two weeks	in two weeks' time

The possessive apostrophe can confuse children. However, the National Literacy Strategy requires its introduction in Year 4 and its revision at this stage. Explain that simple plurals (where no "owning" is involved) do not need apostrophes.

Clauses

A **clause** is part of a sentence. A **clause** must contain a **verb** (a doing or being word). The **main clause** in a sentence makes sense on its own; it can usually be written as a sentence by itself. A **subordinate clause** gives further meaning to the **main clause** but does not make complete sense on its own.

Look at this sentence.

As time went by, the people grew weary of hearing the words of wisdom.

The **main clause** is "the people grew weary of hearing the words of wisdom" – it could be a sentence on its own. The **subordinate clause** is "as time went by" – it is not a complete sentence on its own.

Write down the **main** and **subordinate clauses** in the sentences below.

In a small town, a young man, his wife and the young man's sister all lived together.

main clause: _a young man, his wife and the young man's sister all lived together_

subordinate clause: _In a small town_

Again and again, the people returned to the great tree, but no voice spoke to them.

main clause: _the people returned to the great tree_

two subordinate clauses: _Again and again, but no voice spoke to them_

A short while later, the neglected mango tree lost its leaves and it began to die.

two main clauses: _the neglected mango tree lost its leaves_
it began to die

subordinate clause: _A short while later_

This page features an exercise in identifying main clauses in longer sentences. This can be difficult for less-fluent readers who need encouragement to read words in groups rather than singly. Explain that a clause must contain a verb (otherwise it's a phrase).

Understanding poetry

Read this **poem** aloud.

The Rabbit

We are going to see the rabbit.
We are going to see the rabbit.
Which rabbit, people say?
Which rabbit, ask the children?
Which rabbit?
The only rabbit,
The only rabbit in England,
Sitting behind a barbed-wire fence
Under the floodlights, neon lights,
Sodium lights,
Nibbling grass
On the only patch of grass
In England, in England
(Except the grass by the hoardings
Which doesn't count.)
We are going to see the rabbit
And we must be there on time.

First we shall go by escalator,
Then we shall go by underground,
And then we shall go by motorway
And then by helicopterway,
And the last ten yards we shall have to go
On foot.

And now we are going
All the way to see the rabbit,
We are nearly there,
We are longing to see it,
And so is the crowd
Which is here in thousands
With mounted policemen
And big loudspeakers
And bands and banners,
And everyone has come a long way.
But soon we shall see it
Sitting and nibbling
The blades of grass
On the only patch of grass
In – but something has gone wrong!
Why is everyone so angry,
Why is everyone jostling
And slanging and complaining?

The rabbit has gone,
Yes, the rabbit has gone.
He has actually burrowed down into the earth
And made himself a warren, under the earth,
Despite all these people.
And what shall we do?
What *can* we do?

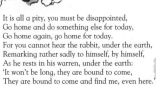

It is all a pity, you must be disappointed,
Go home and do something else for today,
Go home again, go home for today.
For you cannot hear the rabbit, under the earth,
Remarking rather sadly to himself, by himself,
As he rests in his warren, under the earth:
'It won't be long, they are bound to come,
They are bound to come and find me, even here.'

Alan Brownjohn

Listen to your child read the poem. Help your child if he or she finds any parts difficult. This poem is a good example of free verse (unrhymed or irregular verse) that nevertheless has a pattern. Talk about what gives the poem pattern, e.g., the repetition.

Reading and understanding

Reread the **poem** on page 18, then answer the following questions in full sentences.

Is this **poem** about the past, the present or the future? What evidence is there in the poem for your answer?
I can tell this poem is about the future because there is only one patch of grass
left in England and only one rabbit.

Why do you think that this is the only rabbit on the only patch of grass?
I think that there is no room left for grass and so the rabbits have died out
because they had nothing to eat.

What is a hoarding? D
A hoarding is a large board on the side of the road that displays advertisements.

Five ways of travelling are mentioned in the **poem**. What are they? Which is least harmful to the environment?
The five methods of transport in the poem are escalator, underground, motorway,
helicopterway, and on foot. On foot is the least harmful.

Find the **noun** that names the rabbit's home, then write another word for a rabbit's home. D
Remember: A **noun** is a naming word.
In the poem the rabbit's home is called a warren. It can also be called a burrow.

Can you name the wild animals that live in a **sett**, an **earth** and a **holt**? D
A badger lives in a sett, a fox lives in an earth, and a otter lives in a holt.

Why is the rabbit sad?
The rabbit is sad because he is alone and because he can't escape the crowds of
people.

In some places rabbits are regarded as pests. What does this mean?
In some places rabbits eat crops that people have grown.

The questions on this page refer to the poem on page 18. Encourage your child to think about the major issue conveyed by the poem and to form and express opinions on that issue.

Persuasive arguments

Read this example of **informative** and **persuasive** writing.

1 Homes for others
Every living creature has a place where it feels at home. Polar bears are at home in the Arctic; lions are at home in the African grasslands. The place where a creature feels at home is called its natural habitat. You feel at home in your own house. You have safe food to eat and you may know your neighbours, even if you are not friends with all of them. It is the same for all other creatures. Their natural habitat is a place where they and their ancestors have lived for perhaps millions of years. They are used to the climate and the other species in the same habitat. Very often wild creatures can only live in one sort of habitat. Conservationists began by saving species which were threatened by stopping hunting, poaching, or overfishing. Now, people realise that saving a species is not enough. Its home has to be saved as well. Natural habitats are in danger everywhere. When people cut down forests or drain swamps the creatures which lived in those habitats may have nowhere else to go.

2 Why conserve?

We are faced with an important decision. We know that thousands of different species are threatened with becoming extinct. Once they are gone, they will never come back. There are probably thousands more in existence that we don't know about because we haven't discovered them yet. Conservation can save some of these species, but costs money and affects people's lives. Why should we bother with it?

3 Looking after ourselves
We need the other creatures in the biosphere because they provide us with food, building materials, fuel and medicine. However we must use these carefully and sparingly. If we destroy the biosphere because we are greedy or just stupid, then we will die out ourselves. If we look after it, we shall survive, and so will all the other creatures. So conserving the biosphere means looking after ourselves.

From *Endangered Earth* by Jeremy Burgess

What effect do you think the **headings** of the **paragraphs** have on the reader?
The headings clarify what each paragraph is about, emphasising the main points.

Here your child is introduced to informative and persuasive writing. Arguing a case or a point of view and backing it with examples is a useful skill. Help your child realise, however, that such writing is subjective and seldom represents a balanced view.

21 — Writing a summary

Write out as a list the first sentence in each **paragraph** on page 20.

1 *Every living creature* has a place where it feels at home.

2 *We are faced with an important decision.*

3 *We need the other creatures in the biosphere because they provide us with food, clothing, building materials, fuel and medicine.*

Read these sentences again, then **summarise** (write a shortened version of) the writer's argument. Try to write it in 150 words or less, without leaving out any of the main ideas.

Answers may vary

Draw your child's attention to the way the paragraphs in the extract on page 20 each contain a different point. Your child's summary should be a shortened version of the argument that makes sense without reference to the original.

---

22 — More persuasive writing

Reread the **text** on page 20, then answer the following questions in full sentences.

How does the author explain the term **natural habitat**?
The author explains the term natural habitat as a place where a creature feels at home.

The author tells you how you feel in your house – but does he really know? Why do you think he does this?
The author doesn't really know how I feel at home. He assumes I feel good because he wants me to understand how animals feel in their habtat.

The author says that *natural habitats are in danger everywhere*. Is this true or not? Why does he say this?
Not all natural habitats are in danger. The author says that they are to emphasise his point.

How many times does the author use the words **we**, **us** or **ourselves** in paragraphs 2 and 3? Why do you think he does this?
We = 12, us = 1, ourselves = 2. The author uses these words to make the reader feel involved.

The author says that if we look after the biosphere, we will survive and so will all the other creatures. Do you think this is definitely true, or can you think of other possible threats to people and animals?
It is not definitely true that if we look after the biosphere we will survive. Other possible threats include natural disasters and disease.

Write down other **words** or **phrases** (groups of words) that could replace these words in the article without changing its meaning. [D] [T]

poaching *illegal hunting*

extinct *dying out*

biosphere *part of Earth where plants and animals live*

habitat *natural home of a living thing*

conservation *protecting the natural world*

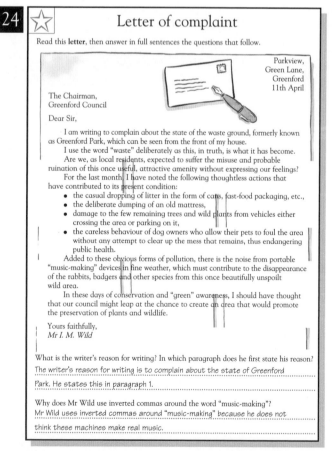

The questions on this page examine the persuasive text (text that deliberately persuades the reader to the writer's view) on page 20 and reveal how it works. You may need to discuss how to approach the answers if your child is unfamiliar with the topic.

---

23 — Conservation dictionary

Make your own **conservation dictionary** by collecting words to do with **conservation** and the prevention of **pollution**. Here are some words to start you off.

pollution   conservation   smog   litter   species

waste   atmosphere   fossil fuels   environment

Now find some more words yourself, and write them here. You may want to use **reference books**, the Internet or **CD-ROMs** to help you. [T]

Answers may vary

Put the **conservation** words in **alphabetical order**, and write a short **meaning** for each one. The **meaning** should be easy to understand. The first one has been done for you. [D]

Word	Meaning
atmosphere	The layer of gases that surrounds the Earth.

Answers may vary

Writing definitions of words will ensure that your child comprehends their meanings, which will aid memory and improve his or her vocabulary. Accept any appropriate and easily understood definitions, and check that the list is in alphabetical order.

---

24 — Letter of complaint

Read this **letter**, then answer in full sentences the questions that follow.

Parkview,
Green Lane,
Greenford
11th April

The Chairman,
Greenford Council

Dear Sir,

I am writing to complain about the state of the waste ground, formerly known as Greenford Park, which can be seen from the front of my house.

I use the word "waste" deliberately as this, in truth, is what it has become. Are we, as local residents, expected to suffer the misuse and probable ruination of this once useful, attractive amenity without expressing our feelings?

For the last month I have noted the following thoughtless actions that have contributed to its present condition:

- the casual dropping of litter in the form of cans, fast-food packaging, etc.,
- the deliberate dumping of an old mattress,
- damage to the few remaining trees and wild plants from vehicles either crossing the area or parking on it,
- the careless behaviour of dog owners who allow their pets to foul the area without any attempt to clear up the mess that remains, thus endangering public health.

Added to these obvious forms of pollution, there is the noise from portable "music-making" devices in fine weather, which must contribute to the disappearance of the rabbits, badgers and other species from this once beautifully unspoilt wild area.

In these days of conservation and "green" awareness, I should have thought that our council might leap at the chance to create an area that would promote the preservation of plants and wildlife.

Yours faithfully,
Mr I. M. Wild

What is the writer's reason for writing? In which paragraph does he first state his reason?
The writer's reason for writing is to complain about the state of Greenford Park. He states this in paragraph 1.

Why does Mr Wild use inverted commas around the word "music-making"?
Mr Wild uses inverted commas around "music-making" because he does not think these machines make real music.

Help your child understand that this letter of complaint is another form of persuasive writing (see page 20). The National Literacy Strategy requires the reading and evaluation of this type of letter. You may wish to look at similar letters in a newspaper.

Reading and understanding

Answer the following questions about the **letter** on page 24.

How does the writer suggest that he is writing on behalf of everyone living in Greenford?
The writer suggests he is writing on behalf of everyone living in Greenford by
using the words "we" and "the local residents".

How does the writer make clear his four main complaints? What are they?
The writer makes his complaints clear by listing them with bullet points.
He complains about litter, dumping, damage to trees and plants by vehicles,
and fouling by pets.

Why does Mr Wild use words such as **casual**, **deliberate**, **thoughtless** and **careless**?
Mr Wild uses these words to emphasise the selfishness of the people who
damage Greenford Park.

The writer is trying to persuade the council to do something. Which words or phrases suggest this?
The words "In these days of conservation and 'green' awareness I should have
thought that our council…" tell us the writer wants the council to help.

Is this just a **letter of complaint**, or does it make any suggestions for improvement? If so, what are they?
The writer suggests that the council makes the Park into an area that will
promote the preservation of plants and wildlife, but he does not say how.

A **rhetorical question** is used to make people think, and an answer is not usually expected. Can you find the **rhetorical question** in this **letter** and write it here?
Are we, as local residents, expected to suffer the misuse and probable ruination
of this once useful, attractive amenity without expressing our feelings?

Do you think this letter will be successful? Why do you think this?
Answers may vary

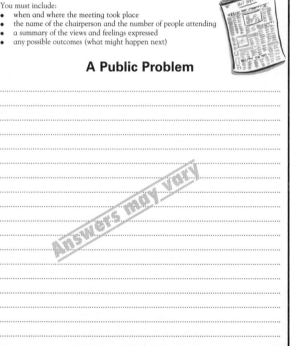

The questions on this page refer to the letter on page 24. These questions should help your child to understand how language can be used to draw attention to a view and also to manipulate the reader.

Information from posters

Read this **poster**. Decide whether or not it will persuade people to take an interest.

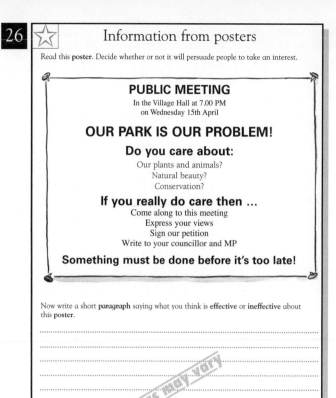

PUBLIC MEETING
In the Village Hall at 7.00 PM
on Wednesday 15th April

OUR PARK IS OUR PROBLEM!

Do you care about:
Our plants and animals?
Natural beauty?
Conservation?

If you really do care then …
Come along to this meeting
Express your views
Sign our petition
Write to your councillor and MP

Something must be done before it's too late!

Now write a short **paragraph** saying what you think is **effective** or **ineffective** about this **poster**.

Answers may vary

Your child's paragraph should comment on how well the poster gains attention, informs and persuades. It may help if you first discuss the meaning of the word *effective*. Check your child's writing for clarity and correct grammar and spelling.

Newspaper report

Imagine you are a reporter working for the local paper. You have been asked to write a brief **report** about what happened at the meeting advertised on the poster on page 26. You have limited space for your report, and the editor has already decided on the headline (see below).

You must include:
- when and where the meeting took place
- the name of the chairperson and the number of people attending
- a summary of the views and feelings expressed
- any possible outcomes (what might happen next)

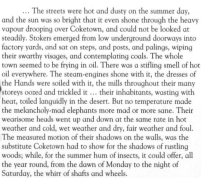

A Public Problem

Answers may vary

The report should include the four elements listed and be in the style of a newspaper report. Try to look at newspapers and letters with your child. Encourage your child to develop a critical eye rather than to accept everything that he or she reads.

Reading a classic novel

In the nineteenth century, some writers wanted their readers to understand more about the lives of others. In those days before television and the Internet, books were one of the most important ways of **persuading** people to think about the rest of the world.

In Chapters 5 and 17 of his novel *Hard Times*, Charles Dickens describes Coketown, an industrial city in the north of England. Read his description of Coketown in these **extracts**.

It was a town of red brick, or of brick that would have been red if the smoke and ashes had allowed it; … It was a town of machinery and tall chimneys, out of which interminable serpents of smoke trailed themselves for ever and ever, and never got uncoiled. It had a black canal in it, and a river that ran purple with ill-smelling dye, and vast piles of building full of windows where there was a rattling and a trembling all day long, and where the piston of the steam-engine worked monotonously up and down, like the head of an elephant in a state of melancholy madness. It contained several large streets all very like one another, and many small streets still more like one another, inhabited by people equally like one another, who all went in and out at the same hours, with the same sound upon the same pavements, to do the same work, and to whom every day was the same as yesterday and tomorrow, and every year the counterpart of the last and the next.

… The streets were hot and dusty on the summer day, and the sun was so bright that it even shone through the heavy vapour drooping over Coketown, and could not be looked at steadily. Stokers emerged from low underground doorways into factory yards, and sat on steps, and posts, and palings, wiping their swarthy visages, and contemplating coals. The whole town seemed to be frying in oil. There was a stifling smell of hot oil everywhere. The steam-engines shone with it, the dresses of the Hands were soiled with it, the mills throughout their many storeys oozed and trickled it … their inhabitants, wasting with heat, toiled languidly in the desert. But no temperature made the melancholy-mad elephants more mad or more sane. Their wearisome heads went up and down at the same rate in hot weather and cold, wet weather and dry, fair weather and foul. The measured motion of their shadows on the walls, was the substitute Coketown had to show for the shadows of rustling woods; while, for the summer hum of insects, it could offer, all the year round, from the dawn of Monday to the night of Saturday, the whirr of shafts and wheels.

You will probably need to help your child read this extract. Reading extracts from classic texts will help familiarise your child with older styles and language and will prepare him or her for reading an entire classic novel in later years.

Reading and understanding

Answer these questions about the **extracts** on page 28.

Charles Dickens uses more detail than many modern writers would. Why do you think this is?

Unfamiliar scenes had to be described in detail because people did not have

TVs or videos showing pictures of them.

Dickens uses many long sentences and repeats words. What effect does this have on the reader?

It conveys the monotony of Coketown life and gives structure and rhythm

to the text. It is like the rhythm of machinery.

Find as many **adjectives** describing **colours**, **sounds** and **smells** as you can. Write them here.
Remember: An **adjective** is a describing word.

red, black, purple, ill-smelling, rattling, trembling, swarthy, stifling, rustling

....

....

Find a **metaphor** for smoke and write it here.
Remember: A writer uses a **metaphor** to describe something as if it were something else.

Interminable serpents

Find a **simile** for a steam-engine and write it here.
Remember: A **simile** is used to compare one thing with another to create an image in the reader's mind. It often includes the words **like** or **as**.

like the head of an elephant in a state of melancholy madness

Here are some of the words that you may have found unfamiliar or difficult. Draw a line to match each one with its meaning. The first one has been done for you. ⬚D

interminable .... very sad
monotonously .... leaked slowly
melancholy .... endless
counterpart .... weakly
wearisome .... same
stokers .... in the same dull way
visage .... furnace feeders
oozed .... boring and tiring
languidly .... face

You may need to discuss some of these questions with your child. You might like to point out that Dickens was a journalist as well as a fiction writer and his novels have an informative and persuasive purpose as well as an entertainment value.

Reading another classic novel

Charles Dickens also wrote *David Copperfield*, a novel about a man's life. As a young boy, David is treated harshly by his stepfather and bullied at school. At the age of ten, he is sent to London to work. Being clever and ambitious, he finds the work very boring. Here, the grown-up David Copperfield describes that particular period in his life.

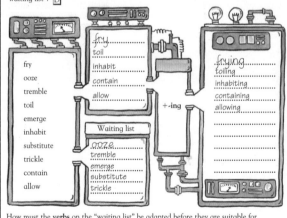

... I became, at ten years old, a little labouring hind in the service of Murdstone and Grinby.

Murdstone and Grinby's warehouse was at the water side. It was down in Blackfriars ... it was the last house at the bottom of a narrow street, curving down hill to the river, with some stairs at the end, where people took boats. It was a crazy old house with a wharf of its own, abutting on the water when the tide was in, and on the mud when the tide was out, and literally over-run with rats. Its panelled rooms, discoloured with the dirt and smoke of a hundred years, I dare say; its decaying floors and staircase, the squeaking and scuffling of the old grey rats down in the cellars; and the dirt and rottenness of the place; are things, not of many years ago, in my mind, but of the present instant. They are all before me, just as they were in the evil hour when I went among them for the first time. ...

Murdstone and Grinby's trade was among a good many kinds of people, but an important branch of it was the supply of wines and spirits to certain packet ships. ... I think there were some among them that made voyages both to the East and West Indies. I know that a great many empty bottles were one of the consequences of this traffic, and that certain men and boys were employed to examine them against the light, and reject those that were flawed, and to rinse and wash them. When the empty bottles ran short, there were labels to be pasted on full ones, or corks to be fitted to them, or seals to be put upon the corks, or finished bottles to be packed in casks. All this work was my work, and of the boys employed upon it I was one.

Name the **narrator** of this part of the story. ⬚D

David Copperfield

Explain the difference between a **narrator** and an **author**. ⬚D

The author is the person who writes the book, and the

narrator is the character in the book who tells the story.

....

On this page your child reads a second extract by Charles Dickens. Where necessary, help with the reading of the text and the implications of the questions. Encourage your child to compare David's childhood with his or her own.

Reading and understanding

Answer these questions about the **extract** on page 30.

The third **paragraph** describes the kind of work that the men and boys did. Can you explain briefly what it was?

The men and boys inspected bottles, rinsed and washed them. They also

pasted on labels, fitted corks and seals, and packed the bottles.

Can you complete these **old words** and **phrases** from the extract? They match the meanings of the **modern words** given below. ⬚D

Modern word	Old word
next to	ab**utting**
rotting	de**caying**
now	of the p**resent** **instant**
journeys	vo**yage**s
a lot of	a g**reat** m**any**
results	co**nsequence**s
damaged	f**lawed**
put on	put **upon**

A **hind** was a servant who lived in a house belonging to the master or mistress. Why is this word used in the first sentence?

The word "hind" was used in the first sentence so that the reader knows

David Copperfield's position in the company.

Do you think this **description** gives the reader a good idea of the way David felt? What words can you think of to describe his feelings about his life and work at this time?

The description gives a good idea of David's feelings. He felt the work was

hard, boring and depressing.

You may like to tell your child that Dickens' family went through a period of poverty when he was a child. Use this as a starting point to talk about the influence of a writer's personal experience on his or her writing.

The word factory

Imagine that there is a machine that adds **-ing** to verbs. Some **verbs** will be unsuitable for this machine unless they have been adapted.
Remember: A **verb** is a doing or being word.

Operate the machine by separating the unsuitable **verbs** from the batch and putting them on the "waiting list". Then put the remaining **verbs** through the machine. The machine has already transformed one **verb** from the batch and put another on the "waiting list". ⬚D

fry
toil
inhabit
contain
allow

fry
ooze
tremble
toil
emerge
inhabit
substitute
trickle
contain
allow

Waiting list
ooze
tremble
emerge
substitute
trickle

+ -ing

frying
toiling
inhabiting
containing
allowing

How must the **verbs** on the "waiting list" be adapted before they are suitable for the machine?

The words on the "waiting list" must have their final **e** removed before they

are ready for the machine.

Write the **verbs** from the "waiting list" as they will appear after they have been processed.

oozing, trembling, emerging, substituting, trickling

This page reinforces one of the spelling rules introduced on page 3 (about how words ending in *-e* are changed when *-ing* is added). Encourage your child to think of other verbs to put through the machine or to invent new machines, e.g., adding *-ful*, *-y*, etc.

Clauses

A **clause** is part of a sentence. A **clause** must contain a **verb** (a doing or being word). The **main clause** in a sentence makes sense on its own; it can usually be written as a sentence by itself. A **subordinate clause** gives further meaning to the **main clause** but does not make complete sense on its own.

Look at this sentence.

As time went by, the people grew weary of hearing the words of wisdom.

The **main clause** is "the people grew weary of hearing the words of wisdom" – it could be a sentence on its own. The **subordinate clause** is "as time went by" – it is not a complete sentence on its own.

Write down the **main** and **subordinate clauses** in the sentences below.

In a small town, there was a small house in which lived a young man, his wife, and the young man's sister.

main clause: ....

....

subordinate clause: ....

They returned to the great tree again and again, hoping to hear the words that would ease their misery.

main clause: ....

subordinate clause: ....

....

As the days passed, the unwatered, uncared for mango tree started drying up and its leaves began to fall.

two **main clauses:** ....

....

subordinate clause: ....

Understanding poetry

Read this **poem** aloud.

The Rabbit

We are going to see the rabbit.
We are going to see the rabbit.
Which rabbit, people say?
Which rabbit, ask the children?
Which rabbit?
The only rabbit,
The only rabbit in England,
Sitting behind a barbed-wire fence
Under the floodlights, neon lights,
Sodium lights,
Nibbling grass
On the only patch of grass
In England, in England
(Except the grass by the hoardings
Which doesn't count.)
We are going to see the rabbit
And we must be there on time.

First we shall go by escalator,
Then we shall go by underground,
And then we shall go by motorway
And then by helicopterway,
And the last ten yards we shall have to go
On foot.

And now we are going
All the way to see the rabbit,
We are nearly there,
We are longing to see it,
And so is the crowd
Which is here in thousands
With mounted policemen
And big loudspeakers
And bands and banners,
And everyone has come a long way.
But soon we shall see it
Sitting and nibbling
The blades of grass
On the only patch of grass
In – but something has gone wrong!
Why is everyone so angry,
Why is everyone jostling
And slanging and complaining?

The rabbit has gone,
Yes, the rabbit has gone.
He has actually burrowed down into the
    earth
And made himself a warren, under the
    earth,
Despite all these people.
And what shall we do?
What *can* we do?

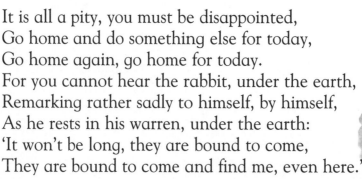

It is all a pity, you must be disappointed,
Go home and do something else for today,
Go home again, go home for today.
For you cannot hear the rabbit, under the earth,
Remarking rather sadly to himself, by himself,
As he rests in his warren, under the earth:
'It won't be long, they are bound to come,
They are bound to come and find me, even here.'

Alan Brownjohn

Reading and understanding

Reread the **poem** on page 18, then answer the following questions in full sentences.

Is this **poem** about the past, the present or the future? What evidence is there in the poem for your answer?

....

....

Why do you think that this is the only rabbit on the only patch of grass?

....

....

What is a hoarding?   D

....

....

Five ways of travelling are mentioned in the **poem**. What are they? Which is least harmful to the environment?

....

....

Find the **noun** that names the rabbit's home, then write another word for a rabbit's home.   D
Remember: A **noun** is a naming word.

....

Can you name the wild animals that live in a **sett**, an **earth** and a **holt**.   D

....

....

Why is the rabbit sad?

....

....

In some places rabbits are regarded as pests. What does this mean?

....

....

Persuasive arguments

Read this example of **informative** and **persuasive** writing.

1 Homes for others

Every living creature has a place where it feels at home. Polar bears
are at home in the Arctic; lions are at home in the African grasslands.
The place where a creature feels at home is called its natural habitat.
You feel at home in your own house. You have safe food to eat and
you may know your neighbours, even if you are not friends with all of
them. It is the same for all other creatures. Their natural habitat is
a place where they and their ancestors have lived for perhaps millions
of years. They are used to the climate and the other species in the
same habitat. Very often wild creatures can only live in one sort
of habitat. Conservationists began by saving species which were
threatened by stopping hunting, poaching, or overfishing. Now, people
realise that saving a species is not enough. Its home has to be saved
as well. Natural habitats are in danger everywhere. When people cut
down forests or drain swamps the creatures which lived in those
habitats may have nowhere else to go.

2 Why conserve?

We are faced with an important decision. We know that thousands
of different species are threatened with becoming extinct. Once they are
gone, they will never come back. There are probably thousands more in
existence that we don't know about because we haven't discovered them
yet. Conservation can save some of these species, but costs money and
affects people's lives. Why should we bother with it?

3 Looking after ourselves

We need the other creatures in the biosphere because they
provide us with food, building materials, fuel and medicine.
However we must use these carefully and sparingly. If we destroy
the biosphere because we are greedy or just stupid, then we will
die out ourselves. If we look after it, we shall survive, and so will all
the other creatures. So conserving the biosphere means looking
after ourselves.

From *Endangered Earth* by Jeremy Burgess

What effect do you think the **headings** of the **paragraphs** have on the reader?

....

....

....

Writing a summary

Write out as a list the first sentence in each **paragraph** on page 20.

1 Every living creature ....
....

2 ....

3 ....
....

Read these sentences again, then **summarise** (write a shortened version of) the writer's argument. Try to write it in 150 words or less, without leaving out any of the main ideas.

....

....

....

....

....

....

....

....

....

....

....

....

....

....

....

....

....

More persuasive writing

Reread the **text** on page 20, then answer the following questions in full sentences.

How does the author explain the term **natural habitat**?

....

....

The author tells you how you feel in your house – but does he really know? Why do you think he does this?

....

....

The author says that *natural habitats are in danger everywhere.* Is this true or not? Why does he say this?

....

....

How many times does the author use the words **we**, **us** or **ourselves** in paragraphs 2 and 3? Why do you think he does this?

....

....

The author says that if we look after the biosphere, we will survive and so will all the other creatures. Do you think this is definitely true, or can you think of other possible threats to people and animals?

....

....

Write down other **words** or **phrases** (groups of words) that could replace these words in the article without changing its meaning.   D   T

poaching ....

extinct ....

biosphere ....

habitat ....

conservation ....

Conservation dictionary

Make your own **conservation dictionary** by collecting words to do with **conservation** and the prevention of **pollution**. Here are some words to start you off.

pollution   conservation   smog   litter   species

waste   atmosphere   fossil fuels   environment

Now find some more words yourself, and write them here. You may want to use **reference books**, the **Internet** or **CD-ROMs** to help you. T

....

....

....

Put the **conservation** words in **alphabetical order**, and write a short **meaning** for each one. The **meaning** should be easy to understand. The first one has been done for you. D

Word	Meaning
atmosphere	The layer of gases that surrounds the Earth.

Letter of complaint

Read this **letter**, then answer in full sentences the questions that follow.

Parkview,
Green Lane,
Greenford
11th April

The Chairman,
Greenford Council

Dear Sir,

I am writing to complain about the state of the waste ground, formerly known as Greenford Park, which can be seen from the front of my house.

I use the word "waste" deliberately as this, in truth, is what it has become.

Are we, as local residents, expected to suffer the misuse and probable ruination of this once useful, attractive amenity without expressing our feelings?

For the last month I have noted the following thoughtless actions that have contributed to its present condition:

- the casual dropping of litter in the form of cans, fast-food packaging, etc.,
- the deliberate dumping of an old mattress,
- damage to the few remaining trees and wild plants from vehicles either crossing the area or parking on it,
- the careless behaviour of dog owners who allow their pets to foul the area without any attempt to clear up the mess that remains, thus endangering public health.

Added to these obvious forms of pollution, there is the noise from portable "music-making" devices in fine weather, which must contribute to the disappearance of the rabbits, badgers and other species from this once beautifully unspoilt wild area.

In these days of conservation and "green" awareness, I should have thought that our council might leap at the chance to create an area that would promote the preservation of plants and wildlife.

Yours faithfully,
Mr I. M. Wild

What is the writer's reason for writing? In which paragraph does he first state his reason?

....

....

Why does Mr Wild use inverted commas around the word "music-making"?

....

....

Reading and understanding

Answer the following questions about the **letter** on page 24.

How does the writer suggest that he is writing on behalf of everyone living in Greenford?

....

....

How does the writer make clear his four main complaints? What are they?

....

....

....

Why does Mr Wild use words such as **casual, deliberate, thoughtless** and **careless**?

....

....

The writer is trying to persuade the council to do something. Which words or phrases suggest this?

....

....

Is this just a **letter of complaint,** or does it make any suggestions for improvement? If so, what are they?

....

....

A **rhetorical question** is used to make people think, and an answer is not usually expected. Can you find the **rhetorical question** in this **letter** and write it here?

....

....

Do you think this letter will be successful? Why do you think this?

....

....

....

....

Read this **poster**. Decide whether or not it will persuade people to take an interest.

PUBLIC MEETING
In the Village Hall at 7.00 PM
on Wednesday 15th April

OUR PARK IS OUR PROBLEM!

Do you care about:
Our plants and animals?
Natural beauty?
Conservation?

If you really do care then …
Come along to this meeting
Express your views
Sign our petition
Write to your councillor and MP

Something must be done before it's too late!

Now write a short **paragraph** saying what you think is **effective** or **ineffective** about this **poster**.

....

....

....

....

....

....

....

....

Newspaper report

Imagine you are a reporter working for the local paper. You have been asked to write a brief **report** about what happened at the meeting advertised on the poster on page 26. You have limited space for your report, and the editor has already decided on the headline (see below).

You must include:
- when and where the meeting took place
- the name of the chairperson and the number of people attending
- a summary of the views and feelings expressed
- any possible outcomes (what might happen next)

A Public Problem

....

....

....

....

....

....

....

....

....

....

....

....

....

....

....

....

Reading a classic novel

In the nineteenth century, some writers wanted their readers to understand more about the lives of others. In those days before television and the Internet, books were one of the most important ways of **persuading** people to think about the rest of the world.

In Chapters 5 and 17 of his novel *Hard Times*, Charles Dickens describes Coketown, an industrial city in the north of England. Read his description of Coketown in these **extracts**.

It was a town of red brick, or of brick that would have been red if the smoke and ashes had allowed it; … It was a town of machinery and tall chimneys, out of which interminable serpents of smoke trailed themselves for ever and ever, and never got uncoiled. It had a black canal in it, and a river that ran purple with ill-smelling dye, and vast piles of building full of windows where there was a rattling and a trembling all day long, and where the piston of the steam-engine worked monotonously up and down, like the head of an elephant in a state of melancholy madness. It contained several large streets all very like one another, and many small streets still more like one another, inhabited by people equally like one another, who all went in and out at the same hours, with the same sound upon the same pavements, to do the same work, and to whom every day was the same as yesterday and tomorrow, and every year the counterpart of the last and the next.

… The streets were hot and dusty on the summer day, and the sun was so bright that it even shone through the heavy vapour drooping over Coketown, and could not be looked at steadily. Stokers emerged from low underground doorways into factory yards, and sat on steps, and posts, and palings, wiping their swarthy visages, and contemplating coals. The whole town seemed to be frying in oil. There was a stifling smell of hot oil everywhere. The steam-engines shone with it, the dresses of the Hands were soiled with it, the mills throughout their many storeys oozed and trickled it … their inhabitants, wasting with heat, toiled languidly in the desert. But no temperature made the melancholy-mad elephants more mad or more sane. Their wearisome heads went up and down at the same rate in hot weather and cold, wet weather and dry, fair weather and foul. The measured motion of their shadows on the walls, was the substitute Coketown had to show for the shadows of rustling woods; while, for the summer hum of insects, it could offer, all the year round, from the dawn of Monday to the night of Saturday, the whirr of shafts and wheels.

Reading and understanding

Answer these questions about the **extracts** on page 28.

Charles Dickens uses more detail than many modern writers would. Why do you think this is?

....

....

Dickens uses many long sentences and repeats words. What effect does this have on the reader?

....

....

Find as many **adjectives** describing **colours, sounds** and **smells** as you can.
Write them here.
Remember: An **adjective** is a describing word.

....

....

....

Find a **metaphor** for smoke and write it here.
Remember: A writer uses a **metaphor** to describe something as if it were something else.

....

Find a **simile** for a steam-engine and write it here.
Remember: A **simile** is used to compare one thing with another to create an image in the reader's mind. It often includes the words **like** or **as**.

....

Here are some of the words that you may have found unfamiliar or difficult. Draw a line to match each one with its meaning. The first one has been done for you. D

interminable	very sad
monotonously	leaked slowly
melancholy	endless
counterpart	weakly
wearisome	same
stokers	in the same dull way
visage	furnace feeders
oozed	boring and tiring
languidly	face

Reading another classic novel

Charles Dickens also wrote *David Copperfield*, a novel about a man's life. As a young boy, David is treated harshly by his stepfather and bullied at school. At the age of ten, he is sent to London to work. Being clever and ambitious, he finds the work very boring. Here, the grown-up David Copperfield describes that particular period in his life.

... I became, at ten years old, a little labouring hind in the service of Murdstone and Grinby.

Murdstone and Grinby's warehouse was at the water side. It was down in Blackfriars ... it was the last house at the bottom of a narrow street, curving down hill to the river, with some stairs at the end, where people took boats. It was a crazy old house with a wharf of its own, abutting on the water when the tide was in, and on the mud when the tide was out, and literally over-run with rats. Its panelled rooms, discoloured with the dirt and smoke of a hundred years, I dare say; its decaying floors and staircase, the squeaking and scuffling of the old grey rats down in the cellars; and the dirt and rottenness of the place; are things, not of many years ago, in my mind, but of the present instant. They are all before me, just as they were in the evil hour when I went among them for the first time. ...

Murdstone and Grinby's trade was among a good many kinds of people, but an important branch of it was the supply of wines and spirits to certain packet ships. ... I think there were some among them that made voyages both to the East and West Indies. I know that a great many empty bottles were one of the consequences of this traffic, and that certain men and boys were employed to examine them against the light, and reject those that were flawed, and to rinse and wash them. When the empty bottles ran short, there were labels to be pasted on full ones, or corks to be fitted to them, or seals to be put upon the corks, or finished bottles to be packed in casks. All this work was my work, and of the boys employed upon it I was one.

Name the **narrator** of this part of the story. ⬚D

....

Explain the difference between a **narrator** and an **author**. ⬚D

....

....

....

Reading and understanding

Answer these questions about the **extract** on page 30.

The third **paragraph** describes the kind of work that the men and boys did.
Can you explain briefly what it was?

....

....

Can you complete these **old words** and **phrases** from the extract? They match the
meanings of the **modern words** given below. D

Modern word	Old word
next to	ab _ _ _ _ _ g
rotting	d _ _ _ _ _ _ _ g
now	of the p _ _ _ _ _ _ _ i _ _ _ _ _ _ _ t
journeys	vo _ _ _ _ s
a lot of	a gr _ _ t m _ _ _ y
results	co _ _ _ _ _ _ _ _ _ _ s
damaged	f _ _ _ _ _ d
put on	put _ _ _ _ _

A **hind** was a servant who lived in a house belonging to the master or mistress. Why is
this word used in the first sentence?

....

....

Do you think this **description** gives the reader a good idea of the way David felt? What
words can you think of to describe his feelings about his life and work at this time?

....

....

The word factory

Imagine that there is a machine that adds **-ing** to **verbs**. Some **verbs** will be unsuitable for this machine unless they have been adapted.
Remember: A **verb** is a doing or being word.

Operate the machine by separating the unsuitable **verbs** from the batch and putting them on the "waiting list". Then put the remaining **verbs** through the machine.
The machine has already transformed one **verb** from the batch and put another on the "waiting list". D

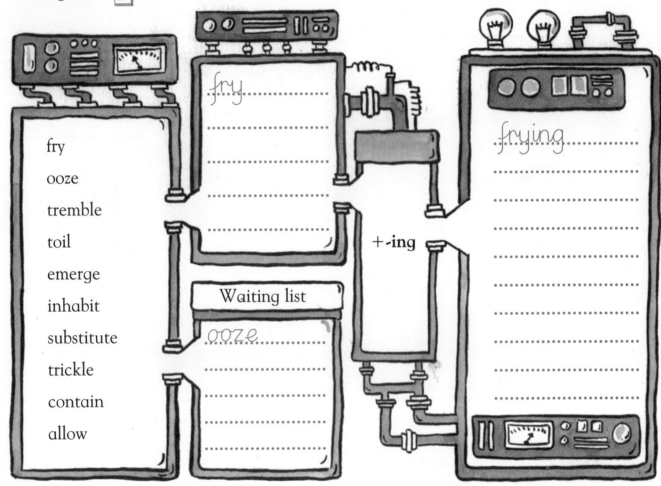

fry
ooze
tremble
toil
emerge
inhabit
substitute
trickle
contain
allow

fry

Waiting list

ooze

+ -ing

frying

How must the **verbs** on the "waiting list" be adapted before they are suitable for the machine?

....

....

Write the **verbs** from the "waiting list" as they will appear after they have been processed.

....

....